Life in PROGRESS

The First Step into the *Left-Hand Path*

The Unknown

Life in Progress

The First Step into the Left-Hand Path
By The Unknown

Edited by Vanessa Ta
Designed by Natalia Junqueira

ISBN 9798884364721
ISBN 9798881144784
ISBN 9798869240897

Copyright© July 2024 by The Unknown

All rights reserved. No part of this book may be reproduced or used in any manner without written permission of the copyright owner except for the use of quotations in a book review. For more information, contact:

obscurity22@yahoo.com
https://www.facebook.com/profile.php?id=100093191436080&mibextid=ZbWKwL
https://www.youtube.com/@TheUnknownLeftHandPath

First paperback edition June 2024

To those who want to escape from
CORRUPTION.

There is nothing more honest than
the results of our actions.

Content

Chapter 1. Originate

Chapter 2. Our Existence

Chapter 3. The Solution to Problem-Solving

Chapter 4. Disposable

Chapter 5. Awareness

Chapter 6. Possession

Chapter 7. The Grandest Stage

Chapter 8. False Hope

Chapter 9. The Result

Chapter 1
ORIGINATE

Contributing with what lies in the air
Only in a mind that appears to be open
It's the density of what's happening
The induction of the outside
A whole new way to live
A change in the way of learning
Because nothing makes sense
While being controlled by your own **prison**
Adapt your mind to where it's capable of having a vision
That you have been hiding from

Then you will see a way
Life has a reason for you to stay
Contrast in the world
To help you understand the unexplained
And live without a name or a face
The shape that divides you from the ideal level
The only change to distract you from the lies of the
truth
By believing in yourself
To disconnect from the prison that holds
you
The change you will originate

There you will restore all the things that protect you from
This so-called **world** and its **wisdom**
A chance to survive without fear of being brought down
It will only save you
If you want to save yourself

RLD

OOM

Chapter 2
OUR EXISTENCE

Are we proud of who we are becoming?
Our short lives don't give us a name for our existence
Does the importance of what we stand for give us a true
purpose?
And do we have control?
Is the truth about our lives just a bunch of bullshit?
Would faith protect us all?
We have strength but is it in us?
Does fate have any sense of direction?
Because humanity seems to never learn
What life considers a lesson

So what if our focus has to be changed?
Will our lives ever be the same?
And if it wasn't enough to be saved
Will the chance ever come again?
Because our success loses strength in our world
And our failures change all that we know
So maybe life will let us go

This might be our chance to create a better method
To provide us with an establishment that will show us the right way to live

What if a chance came unannounced and showed us
everything?
And we denied everything we saw
Because our ignorance seemed so much easier
Then all sorts of shit starts taking control
And it all started to make sense
All the ways we lived our lives became our punishment
Suddenly everything started to come along
And everyone is still in denial
Certainly we should already have known
That our conditional realization chose to cancel all creation

Our existence will then die
And then what does blame come to solve?
When there's no one to blame because we are all guilty
All the ways we could have solved things
But we decided to never know

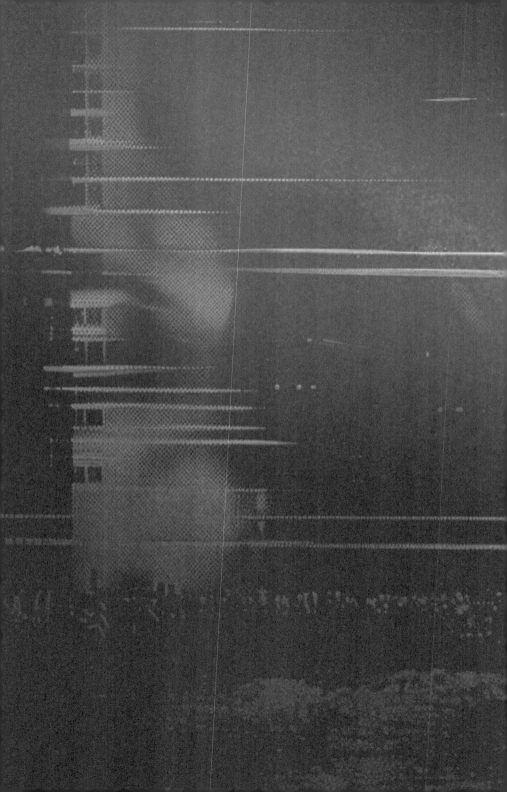

Chapter 3
THE SOLUTION TO PROBLEM-SOLVING

Right and wrong is what defines the way we all think
Every choice we make has a reason
And every decision is an action with a reaction we have to face
It's either for pleasure or it's for pain
So there has never been a single person
That has acted on any decision
Without ever having a good enough reason
It doesn't matter whether it's right or wrong
It made sense to them

And judgment is so persistent with the ordinance
There's no requirement to understand the human mind
They have to call in a specialist to cope with the fact we all live different lives
Otherwise they're ready to shoot you where you're standing
And end it by saying you have crossed the line
There's so much more that we don't even know
It's not even written in the paperwork
Now we all have the numbers to build a movement
But no one seems to speak and lead in the present time
You are just too afraid to start a parade of allegiance
Because the judgment is so short-sighted
And you are aware of every possible outcome

Well it's time to face that we are all human
There are no more mistakes as long as we are learning
Because all our intentions are the desire to get even
And to value the beauty that life has given
It's just the way it balances out
And no one can call that an opinion
Because we are only human
Now if you want to call it a defeat
So you can stay in your homes
Well I'm not going to take this shit
Even if I have to stand on my own
I'm going to show them that every action has a meaning
And every reason is worth explaining
There's a line drawn that overrides their reasons

So let's have a war that will solve everything
Let's fight with everybody else's lives
And see who's winning
It's the way it all balances out
It's the solution to problem-solving

Chapter 4
DISPOSABLE

For every life there will be death
A continuous cycle in various ways
We are all predators attacking the prey
Causing death in order to live
Adaptation, evolution, karma, and recycling
Will cover the entire process

And the purpose is to support the nature within
When it all began
It's the survival of the strong
With billions of years holding on
Rebuilding to be destroyed
A perfect design to oppose an end

Existence is **Nature**'s layout to outlive
Out with the old and then the new will be in
With the concept of the biodegradables
Consistently working to continue the revolution
Because everything is disposable
Supporting the balance from being overwhelmed
Otherwise life will consume itself
Adaptation, evolution, karma, and recycling
Is the only answer
And the purpose is to support the nature within

It's right in front of us
How can we be so blind to it?
And it's obvious
As the seasons change
We can clearly see

Spring is a time for everything to begin
While Summer allows everything to be free to live
And Fall is the time for everything to change
Where Winter brings all the life to hibernate

Just to start all over again

Supporting the balance from being overwhelmed

Chapter 5
AWARENESS

Descend into the quicksand of yourself

Invert your perception inside then look out

Acknowledge the freedom outside by the sound

And these senses link us to movement

Without guidance, without restriction, and without question

The only purpose is to learn and move forward

To preserve life through your conscious

A balance of pain and pleasure

And recognize the concept of survival

To nourish your instincts and desires

So experience this new world out in the wild
Discovering new ways of knowing about yourself
And how you fit in
With a combination of

consciousness,

desire,

instinct,

and

intelligence

So see it, hear it, smell it, touch it, and taste it
To enhance your awareness to the highest extent
And discover new ways by observing other life
It doesn't always have to be done your way
Move on and evolve

Just remember it's your life

It's your **choice**

You're in control

With an entire world to discover

# Chapter 6
POSSESSION

It's all for you
It's all for you, it's all for YOU
At one time everything was for everyone
Until one day it became all yours
You put up your walls to close it in
And then gave it a name
With a list of rules
This way of thinking became so contagious
Soon everyone started hoarding theirs
So we might as well just fall in
Into obsession with possessions
So it all becomes our supply and demand

Now it's raining endless debt on consumers

For those who are collecting

And believe it will give them power

This mentality won't take you anywhere

Besides turning into a slave to materials

That will one day convince you

That you are one

Live or die over things that get left behind

If that's considered living

And this is where it takes us

Was it all worth it?

In the end

It will continue to consume the consumer

Until it's all owned by only one owner

So who are you?
Because it's all for **you**
It's all for **you**, it's all for **YOU**
At this point it already reached inflation
We need to make a stand
That this is it
There has to be destruction
To get rid of all this bullshit weighing down our head
We need to think and break away
From a hold possession has on everyone
Let's knock down all of these walls
Let's burn everything you call your home
You're the one with everything
That once belonged to everyone

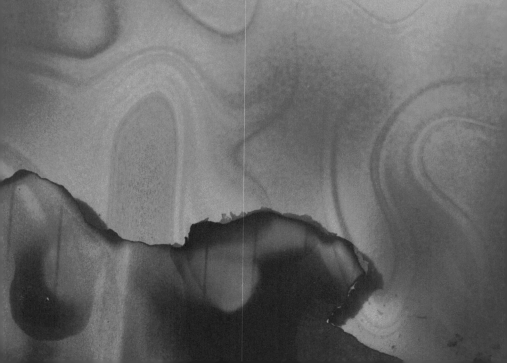

How do you get such ferocity?
To own everything entirely
Because we all end with nothing material
Only the people that made you whole
Will give you any real meaning
Did you ever love anyone besides all of your possessions?
So what's the point of having everything?
When you're left with no one

You become so empty

With no reason to move on
And that would be a destruction
Of your world alone
So what's the point of living?
When you're done
Owning everything including everyone
You've become God

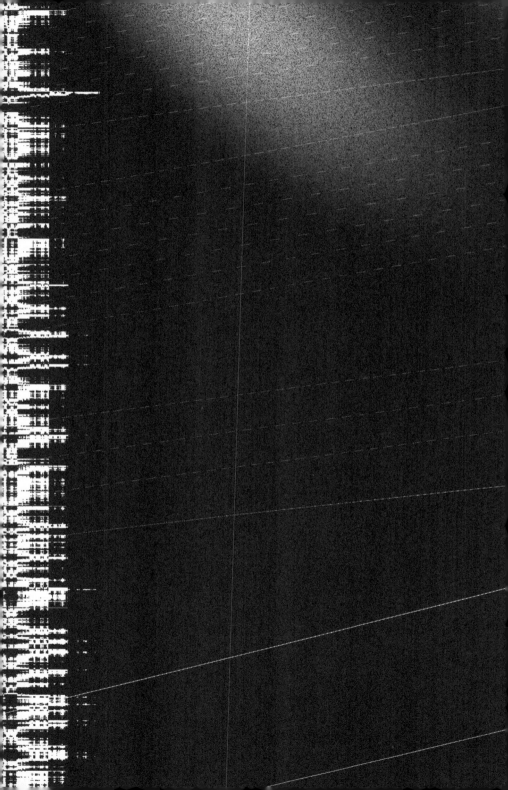

Chapter 7
THE GRANDEST STAGE

Now that I have your attention
Allow me to explain the pollution of ignorance within the corruption
So try to grasp this one
Because I'm going to go deep inside your mind where it resides
And I want to expose what lies behind the curtain
Upon the grandest stage of religion and how it all began
Starting with the three points ruled by manipulation
So it will remain in constant motion until the end
While a triangle will start the function of this diagram
Using government and law to create the perfect foundation
And religion will become universal from support within this rotation

To become a system that's controlling an entire population
Those who want to live within the protection it will provide them
Because this new way of living creates weakness through
                                              disposition
    Leaving behind the natural way by making it forbidden
      To become distracted by starting a cycle of questions
        Amongst all of the children who will become the next
                                                generation
To lead the way into change
When dependency creates the mentality of a slave
The perfect type of mind that you can shape
Even emotions can play a part in this game
You can say whatever you want to say
Regardless if it changes their distinction
after they come to this place
It provides a way to escape

By leading them far far away from the wild
With a promise to compromise
                                        Leaving behind what was before
    And providing everything they will need to keep them alive
            But nothing is given away without labor being implied
                    And those who put in will partially rise
                        While leaving no room to disagree in the eyes
                              Of those who will leave you to die
If you don't comply
Allowing fear to become more complex
within the fragile mind
So in order to stay alive you will now have to pay the price
With costs of inflation that always lead to a bribe
Why did you ever buy into believing in the design?
When liberation can take an entire lifetime

Providing the all mighty dollar from your labor before you die
Not exactly leaving a lot of room to decide
Because you've been living in a lie the entire time
A lie to persuade the cause and effect of humankind
The plan is to keep you weak with ignorance from the corruption that's buried deep within your head
It alters the way of your comprehension
Before getting a chance to understand the way it is
The second you're born it will wait in position
Through the guidance of your parents and education
Who will force you to believe in the system
Tempting you to do the things
It teaches you to be against

The ultimate mind fuck

Blaming everything on everyone to force us into separation
The deprived and the privileged
Divided within the churches and prisons
Creating hate over differences
To lead us into prejudice and discrimination
Causing destruction under false confusion

Because it's all a bunch of **bullshit**

You've become nothing more than sheep
Following the directions from an egotistical, lethargic, and tyrant shepard
Being distracted and misguided away from the balance of your nature
Since when did life start asking a bunch of questions that needed to be answered?

What's the point of living if you're not getting something in return?
While creating indulgence with everyone
Using possessions as a distraction
So everyone grows to never be satisfied
Why should we even live if we're just going to die?
And so it begins with religion

Chapter 8
FALSE HOPE

This goes out to those who want to make
a difference in the world
Well it's been going on as long as differences
have been compared
And it's clear that the struggle has always been here
Existence can't exist without its persistence
To change the result before it could even begin
It's a vicious cycle that leads to tomorrow's future problems
Retaliation is Nature's reaction
against its former place in change
So survival can become a natural motivation
to prevent any waste
Disposable properties are all within accordance to be
recycled again
In a form of creation to exist without an end

To become is to be given a way to be free
And not weighed down and built up
without a breakdown to configure a relief
But then an unnatural display interfered with this way to agree
Disguised as a solution for a problem that didn't even happen
All along the problem was the solution
to be conditioned and unaware
So **beware** ...

With the movies, TV shows, music, and literature
People have expressed how the world is supposed to be
Reminding us that it can be better
But it never will
As long as they show that it is possible
Then there is no need for it to happen

There will always be a need to hope for a better world
Without actually having it
That's what makes this world go around
A manipulation believed by everyone
For the greater good that will never be
This is only one example that needs to be changed
Until all hope is lost

        And we find another way
        Now think
        We need to stop trying to fix the world
        And start fixing ourselves

Hope is pointless in a world that can take care of itself
Hope spends money on cures that will never happen
Even if they have always been there
Hope takes away the possibility for change
to even take place

Hope ends before it begins

And without a purpose to even exist

Without a way to change or be replaced

HOPE

will never mean anything as the result is a mistake

Chapter 9
THE RESULT

It's time to face the result of our existence
By accepting this world for what it is
The very Hell we've been convinced would be the outcome
If we ever went against this poisonous system
Has become the result of our relations within its creation
So now you're expected to do the best you can
In this illusion that we are all trapped in
There is nothing more honest than the results of our actions
This reality is nothing more than a material existence
Waiting for the next possibility to become a little bit stronger

A way to evolve through all the unnatural
corruption and ignorance
Because humankind desires
to have the power of creation in
the palm of their hand
But only being allowed to make this reality
completely based on manipulation
An endless hole where we are all continuously falling
So now it's time to overcome this greatest challenge
And to evolve when we finally reach the end
Where there's no right or wrong
No truth or lies
No innocence or guilt
No Heaven or Hell
And no hope for any god to save us all
Because they are all man-made concepts
that have evolved

But everyone had a right to believe
in it for themselves
Because the result focuses on everything
in the universe
The result is what you get out of your life
So live it for yourself
The result accepts everyone for who they are
And how they fit in
The result will always benefit everyone's needs
Because that's how everything ends
before it will begin again
Everything we do is for the result
And we have always followed the result
without even realizing it
I'm just making it obvious

People will even feel better about death
because of the result
What you don't get out of this life
You will in the next
And that is the point of the result
Because you can't escape it
no matter what you believe in
You're in it whether
you like it or not
It's inevitable
Everything is the result of itself
Reality will always be just materials
Until everyone sees it for themselves
You can't understand pain
Until you've felt all the pain life has to offer
You can't understand pleasure
Until you've felt all the pleasure life has to offer

Once your flesh dies
Your soul desires continued existence
To learn more
Just like in flesh
How we seek more of everything
We seek more in spirit
Desiring life more and more until it's fulfilled
Then and only then you will have your spiritual birth
To become your true self
A spirit in flesh
When life and death mingle into a
slow vibration for all
existence
The highest of high
And the lowest of low
Total perfection without the void

Now your soul can finally experience
all of the senses
Without being controlled
Because you understand life for what it is
It's like charging your soul's battery
And it's not fulfilled till it reaches 100%
So as a result we are left to believe
We've always known this reality as Hell
With many different levels of experience
Life is all about living within this manipulation
To experience all that it has to offer
All of the pain and all of the pleasure
While this reality is full of diversity
Corresponding with their own design
Trying to connect with those
who can help them stabilize
All within their path of understanding

Either you have a slave mentality
or you are free
But freedom in this reality
is a mind game for everyone
And the point of everything
Is to live life to overcome
Any challenges you may experience
Because everyone is in it for themselves
Including those closest to you
So remember life is about
experiencing every level
Until your soul has been fulfilled
To become your true self
And achieve a spiritual birth

Otherwise you will continue in
the cycle of materials
Unless you fix this reality
By accepting the people within it
Because unnatural ignorance
prevents humanity to advance
And destruction is the result
of unnatural corruption within
unnatural ignorance
Because the natural is so powerful
It will leave this world
of manipulation speechless
Now you will need time to adjust

BONUS
Chapter 10
THE SKELETON OF CREATION

A DEEPER LOOK INTO THE DESCRIPTION OF CREATION

Woven within the thickness of nothing
The darkest of all comprehension before expanding
Begins to consist of energy generating in a pattern
Going with and against
Challenging the motion of a singular component
Corresponding with the wavelength
By composing into a shape
From vibrations coming from in-depth
Then drastically meeting into the vertex
To create a dimension
To become the skeleton of creation
The outline of existence
While the pattern forms a diagram
Corresponding
By folding over repeatedly without an end

To force the pressure against itself
To create a multitude of singularities
Corresponding in unison
Are all within the blueprint
So corresponding
Puts them right in their place
So woven within the thickness of nothing
The darkest of all comprehension after some expanding
Consists of energy generating in patterns
Going with and against
Challenging the motion of total opposites
Corresponding with the wavelengths
By composing into different shapes

From vibrations coming from in-depth
Then drastically meeting into the opposing vertex
To create another dimension
To become the skeleton of creation
The outline of existence
While the patterns continue to form the diagram
Corresponding
By folding over repeatedly without an end
Forcing more pressure against themselves
To create a multitude of other singularities
Corresponding in unison
Are all within the same blueprint
So corresponding
Puts them right in their place
And so and so on
To create what we all know as space

Also available from The Unknown, Author:

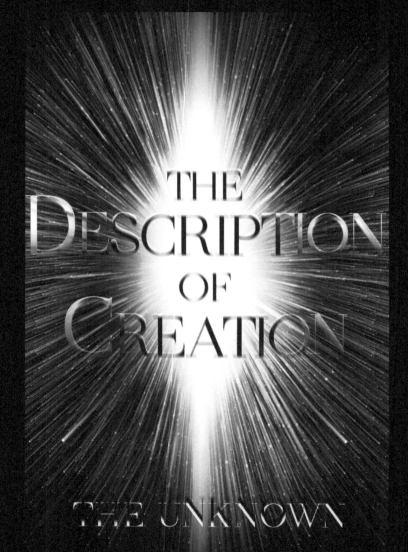

MESSAGE OF THE AUTHOR

Believe in yourself. And follow the results of your actions, so you can make a difference in your life. The rest of the world will follow.